CHAPTER 1
AND PYX CHAMBER
WESTMINSTER ABBEY

Warwick Rodwell

In 1253, as King Henry III's Chapter House neared completion, it was described as 'beyond compare' and ranked amongst the great achievements of Gothic architecture. One of the largest English chapter houses, it served not only as the formal meeting place for the monks of Westminster Abbey, but, uniquely, had an additional role as the assembly place for the king's 'Great Court', the predecessor of the English Parliament. A crypt beneath the Chapter House contained a royal treasury, which extended into an adjacent room known as the Pyx Chamber.

At the dissolution of the abbey in 1540, the Chapter House and Pyx Chamber were used as a repository for important government records, becoming the precursor of the Public Record Office, a use which continued until 1863. Following a major restoration by the great Victorian architect Sir George Gilbert Scott in 1866–72, the building was opened to the general public.

On account of their dual role for secular and religious functions, the Chapter House and Pyx Chamber have always been royal property. Today they are administered on behalf of the Crown by English Heritage.

CONTENTS

Published by English Heritage
23 Savile Row, London W1S 2ET
© English Heritage 2002
First published by English Heritage 2002
Photography by the English Heritage Photographic Unit
and copyright English Heritage unless otherwise stated

Edited by Kate Jeffrey
Designed by Pauline Hull
Plan by Richard Morris

Printed in England by St Ives Westerham Press
C50 7/02 ISBN 1 85074 791 1
Visit our website at www.english-heritage.org.uk

*Previous page: Floor tiles in the Chapter House
showing the salmon of St Peter*

*Below: The Last Judgement wall paintings on the
south-east wall of the Chapter House. The portrait
faces may represent members of parliament*

A HISTORY OF THE CHAPTER HOUSE AND PYX CHAMBER

The chapter house was the administrative heart of any Benedictine abbey. It was the place where the monks met every morning for special prayers, and to hear readings from the Rule of St Benedict. Essential business was also conducted, such as the allocation of duties for the day, and discipline was meted out. Westminster was the king's principal palace, and the abbey was his own foundation and dependency. Consequently the Chapter House had a unique additional role as a secular meeting place and the king had the unchallengeable right to use its buildings for his own purposes.

When Henry III began his long reign in 1216 Westminster Abbey was an early Romanesque building, erected in the mid-eleventh century by Edward the Confessor. In 1246 Henry pulled down the eastern parts of the church and began to reconstruct them in the new Gothic style that he had so much admired in France. He intended also to rebuild the cloister

and conventual buildings, a scheme that was not fully realised. However, he demolished part of the east cloister range, including the old chapter house, thus making way for the magnificent new structure which still stands today.

Work on the Chapter House may have begun as early as 1246, and by 1249 it was sufficiently advanced for a new timber lectern to be commissioned from the Flemish carver John of St Omer. By 1253 the masonry shell was complete, and canvas was bought as a temporary filling for the windows. It was probably in that year that Matthew Paris, a chronicler from St Albans, saw the work in progress and observed that the king had built 'a Chapter House beyond compare'. The project was carried out under the supervision of Master Henry de Reins, Keeper of the King's Works, and was probably finished around 1255.

During Henry III's reign, the king's council of feudal lords met increasingly at Westminster, and an appropriate

Incense-bearing angels on the inner entrance to the Chapter House

Henry III's tomb effigy in Westminster Abbey

Engraving of the undercroft or 'crypt' published in Gleanings from Westminster Abbey *by George Gilbert Scott (1863)*

Detail of the stained glass window above the inner entrance showing Elizabeth I

venue was needed. It had to be not only functional but also awe-inspiring. Henry chose his new Chapter House as a venue for his councils, and the first secular assembly there is recorded as having taken place in March 1257. This was effectively the beginning of the English Parliament. By the 1330s, the Lords met separately from the knights and burgesses, who united to form the 'Commons'. The latter met sporadically in the Chapter House until 1395. Meanwhile, the monks complained bitterly that meetings of the Commons intruded into their life of quiet contemplation, and that the stamping and shuffling of feet was wearing out the pavement in the Chapter House. Meetings of the Commons were then transferred to the abbey's refectory, where they continued until 1547, before being given their own permanent chamber in the Palace of Westminster.

The crypt below the Chapter House, and the adjacent room in the cloister, known as the Pyx Chamber, were used as royal 'Wardrobe' treasuries. A noteworthy incident occurred in 1303 when an unsuccessful merchant, Richard de Podelicote, broke into the Wardrobe treasury with the assistance of a stonemason and the collaboration of several monks. He stole a considerable quantity of royal treasure, but was apprehended and hanged.

Under King Henry VIII and his Chancellor Thomas Cromwell, the abbeys of England were systematically dismantled between 1536 and 1540. From its dissolution in 1540 Westminster Abbey ceased to have any monastic function. In the reign of Elizabeth I it gained a new identity as a 'collegiate church' under direct royal patronage, which it has retained to this day. However, the new dean and canons never used the Chapter House: instead it was taken over for the storage of royal records, mainly those associated with the Exchequer. To accommodate the records, timber presses (shelves) were constructed around the walls, and these afforded some protection to the medieval paintings, which might otherwise have been entirely lost. In the eighteenth century, pressure on space resulted in the construction of an internal gallery and stairs. The great medieval windows were reduced to Georgian round-headed lights, and much other structural damage was done. Worst of all, in 1744, the vault was demolished and replaced by a flat ceiling. The tile pavement was, however, protected beneath a suspended timber floor.

The Chapter House and Pyx Chamber had effectively become the

Public Record Office, a function which they continued to serve until 1863. Subsequently both chambers were left empty and without uses. In 1866-72, at government expense, the Chapter House underwent a massive restoration and was opened to the public as a historic monument. Under the architect Sir George Gilbert Scott, all evidence of use as a record office was swept away, the masonry shell was repaired, the stone vault was reconstructed, the geometrical windows were reinstated and reglazed, and many other acts of restoration carried out with full Victorian vigour. This was a notable example of restoration based on archaeological evidence. The Pyx Chamber was not restored. Today, Chapter House and Pyx Chamber are managed on behalf of the Crown by English Heritage, not by the abbey authorities: this distinction is a reminder of the Chapter House's royal past as meeting place, parliament chamber and record office.

Sir George Gilbert Scott (1809–96), in an 1877 portrait by George Richmond

The Chapter House in use as a public record office, 1807

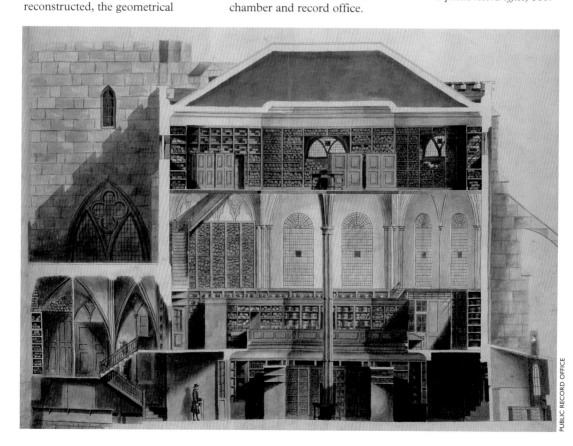

Detail of figures on the inner entrance arch to the Chapter House

The entrance to the vestibule from the cloister

ART AND ARCHITECTURE

The Chapter House complex extends south from the church transept, down the east side of the Great Cloister. It consists of four structural elements: outer vestibule, inner vestibule, the chapter house proper, and its sub-vault or 'crypt'. Above the vestibule lay the monks' dormitory, reached by the 'day stairs' which were sandwiched between the vestibule and the Pyx Chamber. The stone used in the building is mostly from the Reigate area of Surrey, but Purbeck marble from Dorset was employed for capitals, shafts and some other details. A small amount of hard chalk, from Totternhoe, Bedfordshire was also used for fine carving.

In 1377 flying buttresses were added around the exterior to provide extra support for the vault.

THE OUTER VESTIBULE

This vaulted passage is entered from the cloister through elaborate twin doorways, which would have been secured by heavy wrought-iron grilles where the glass doors and Victorian iron gates are today. Above the

entrance are three statues supported on stone corbels. Inside, the vestibule is now occupied by the English Heritage shop. The ceiling is low because it has to pass under the dormitory (now the Chapter Library), and is divided into three bays along its length. Down the centre is a row of Purbeck marble columns which define two processional corridors corresponding to the twin doorways. The southern (right-hand) half of the vault is original, but the northern half was substantially renewed in the nineteenth century. The vestibule served as a lobby or waiting room, and there are stone benches along its side walls.

In the eastern bay are two doors: that on the left opens into St Faith's Chapel (originally a sacristy, or place for storing sacred vessels and vestments), while the other leads into what is now an office under the monastic day stairs. This formerly gave access to the Pyx Chamber, but the way through was blocked in the fourteenth century. The oak door which hangs here is one of the oldest in Britain: dating from the eleventh century, it was later cut down for reuse in this position. The inner face (originally the outside) was once covered with hide and ornamental ironwork, and it is one of a handful of doors around which 'Daneskin' legends have grown up. However, the hide covering was not the skin of a flayed Dane, but that of a cow.

THE INNER VESTIBULE

This taller, vaulted space contains a flight of nine steps leading up to the Chapter House. It served as an entrance porch and 'overflow' space for large assemblies, and there are benches along the side walls. Like the outer vestibule, it has twin doorways and there would have been wrought-iron gates where the elaborate Victorian ones now are. The floor is paved with encaustic tiles (see page 11), mostly nineteenth-century copies of medieval designs. The unusual brass heating grilles are also based on medieval tile designs.

There are two American memorials in the vestibule. The stained-glass windows on the right are by Clayton and Bell and were introduced in 1893 in memory of James Russell Lowell, American Ambassador to Britain, 1880–85. The depictions include the Pilgrim Fathers landing in New England, St Botolph of Boston (Lincolnshire) and the arms of Harvard University. There is also a memorial plaque to Walter Hines Page, American Ambassador from

Left: Eleventh-century oak door in the outer vestibule, now the entrance to the English Heritage office

American memorials in the inner vestibule

1913 to 1918, who is described as 'the friend of Britain in her sorest need'. The glazing of the windows on the left dates from 1951.

THE CHAPTER HOUSE

Another twin doorway opens into the magnificent octagonal chamber which was created as the setting for meetings of both the abbey's chapter and secular councils. The soaring vault is supported on a slender central column of Purbeck marble. Aspects of the design were derived from Amiens Cathedral and the Sainte Chapelle in Paris, but the plan of the structure is peculiarly English: Westminster is part of a series of grand circular and polygonal chapter houses which began with Worcester and Lincoln.

The entrance is lavishly enriched with sculpture and the side walls contain huge windows, each of four lights with geometrical tracery. Below sill level, the walls are punctuated with blind arcading, forming a series of thirty-seven shallow recesses or seats. The five on the east side of the Chapter House are deeper than the others, giving added dignity to the abbot and senior monks. In the back of each recess was a medieval wall painting, and there was also much gilding and colouring on the architectural framework. Running round the chamber in front of the arcading are three tiers of stone steps which provided seating for large assemblies.

The windows would have been filled with thirteenth-century stained glass, but this was all lost by the eighteenth century. New windows, depicting scenes and figures from the history of the abbey and the kingdom, were created by Clayton and Bell in 1882, but these were in turn largely destroyed by German air raids in 1941. Only the west window, above the entrance, survived. The other seven were reglazed by Joan Howson in 1950–51, incorporating salvaged Victorian panels in the north, south and east sides, and new glass in the remainder. The added

Detail of one of the windows that was reglazed after the Second World War

Opposite: The inner entrance arch with the Victorian figure of Christ in Majesty

Left: The reverse of the inner entrance arch with another representation of Christ in Majesty, flanked by incense-bearing angels and the two figures of the Annunciation

The two figures of the Annunciation on the inner entrance to the Chapter House: below, the Archangel Gabriel and right, the Virgin

panels include coats of arms of benefactors and important historical figures associated with the Chapter House from the thirteenth to the nineteenth centuries. The south-west or 'enigma' window is subtly different since it contains numerous tiny scenes and motifs relating to the history of the Second World War. The identifications of the low-level panes are encoded in words (or parts of words) contained in the inscriptions which run across the bottoms of the lights.

Sculpture

The Chapter House complex is adorned with sculptures, notably three large sculpture groups over its succession of doorways. The first group, which can be seen in the cloister walk above the outermost doors, is heavily weathered. The fragmentary centrepiece, which is not original to this position, is a figure of the Virgin and Child; it is flanked by a pair of angels which may have carried candles. The whole area was richly coloured. The second group stood on three corbels (stone supports) in the inner vestibule, but the figures have long since been lost.

The third group is inside the Chapter House itself, above the entrance. Most important are the two great figures of the Annunciation, each 1.8m in height: in a niche on the left is the Archangel Gabriel, who leans back slightly, and on the right is the Virgin Mary with her right hand raised. These

are two of the finest English Gothic sculptures. The figures would have been painted, and Gabriel had wings which have been lost: they were made of wood or metal and were slotted into the statue. Each figure is faced by a pair of incense-bearing angels set into a large trefoil. Finally, filling the central roundel of the arch, is a carving of Christ in Majesty attended by incense-bearing angels. This double-sided sculpture, with images of Christ facing both east and west, is, however, a Victorian insertion: the space was originally open tracery.

The flanks of the doorway and the mouldings of the arch above are intricately decorated with scrolls of foliage and numerous seated figures, which may represent a 'Tree of Jesse'. There are many other small sculptures, such as the capital on the left of the entrance which depicts three lions. The finely carved roof bosses (at the intersections of the ribs of the vault), all nineteenth-century, are a mixture of foliage and figural scenes: looking down upon the entrance are the Virgin and Child.

Floor tiles

The floor of the Chapter House is original and consists of patterned and glazed tiles, laid as a series of 'carpets' running east to west. This is one of the finest medieval tile pavements in England. The designs were created by stamping the pattern into the clay tile and then filling the impression with light-coloured clay, before glazing and firing. The glaze has mostly worn away, but the slightly darker tiles with a glazed surface, which are Victorian replacements, give a good indication of the original appearance of the floor.

Prominently displayed on large tiles running across the Chapter House in two continuous bands are King Henry's arms, the three lions of England; the shields are flanked by centaurs and wyverns (beasts with dragons' heads and serpents' tails). The patterns depicted on the remaining tiles are mostly geometrical, but there are also human figures, animals and fish. A notable feature is a Latin inscription, with each letter contained on one small tile. Although incomplete, the rhyming hexameter begins *Ut rosa flos florum, sic est domus ista domorum* ('As the Rose is the flower of flowers, so this House is the house of houses'); the same phrase occurs in the chapter house at York Minster.

Paintings

Like all important medieval buildings, the walls and decorative mouldings were covered with paint, and very little bare stone would have been exposed. Traces of paint and gilding can be seen in many places, but the most important survival today is the series of paintings contained within the recesses around the Chapter House walls. These are of two periods, both later than the original construction. The earlier

Medieval floor tiles: left, King Henry's arms with the three lions of England; centre, geometrical pattern based on the tracery of a rose window; right, King Edward giving a ring to St John, who is disguised as a pilgrim

Detail of the Last Judgement wall painting on the east wall showing Christ displaying his wounds

Eighteenth-century watercolour of the Last Judgement wall paintings

paintings were given by Brother John of Northampton, a monk of the abbey from 1375/6–1404. They represent the Apocalypse and the Last Judgement and may have been commissioned in the 1390s, when the monks finally succeeded in ousting the House of Commons from the Chapter House. The second series of paintings, dating from the late fifteenth century, comprises birds and beasts which were added at the bottoms of the recesses, below the earlier scheme. The artists are unknown.

The Last Judgement

This large painting is on the east wall of the Chapter House, directly opposite the entrance. It runs continuously behind the freestanding shafts that support the five bays of wall arcading and is so arranged that one major figure appears to fill the back of each seat. Painted in a courtly style, it is a highly finished scene, with gold leaf used to embellish haloes, crowns and jewels. In the centre (the abbot's seat) Christ displays the wounds in his hands: he is robed in crimson and sits on the arc of Heaven with the globe beneath his feet. Beside him are angels in white robes, holding the instruments of the Passion. The flanking arches contain figures of seraphim, holding crowns in their hands, and they are attended by many lesser angels, all with gilded haloes. The figures in the outermost arches are indistinctly preserved, but may have been the Virgin Mary on the north and John the Baptist on the south.

In three of the arches on the south-east side of the chamber (see

plan, inside back cover), flanking the main scene, is an unusual group of figures comprising middle-aged men, rather than the mix of sexes and ages usually depicted in 'doom' or Last Judgement paintings. The men, who are accompanied by ferocious-looking little red angels, have portrait faces, and it has been suggested that they may represent the members of parliament who had recently been evicted from the Chapter House.

The Apocalypse Series

The remaining arches around the walls are filled with a series of panels depicting the Apocalypse. The subject is a series of visions of the end of the world described in the Book of Revelation. The sequence, which begins on the north-west wall beside the entrance and runs clockwise around the chamber, is interrupted by the Last Judgement scenes on the east wall. The style

Detail from the Apocalypse series showing two settings of Christ in Majesty: on the left he is flanked by seven candlesticks and holds seven stars in his hand; on the right he is surrounded by seven lamps and the twenty-four elders playing musical instruments

Detail from the Apocalypse series showing St John on his voyage to the island of Patmos

Musicians in a detail from the Apocalypse of St John

is north German or Netherlandish and is unlike anything else in the abbey.

Under each arch, at the top, is an angel playing a musical instrument, and below are four panels containing single or multiple scenes. The panels are framed with maroon borders, studded with roses or little white dogs. Each panel is accompanied by a long text, inscribed on a piece of parchment which is stuck to the wall. The much later additions of paired beasts, below the Apocalypse panels, are also identified by labels: these include camel ('Kameyl') and crocodile ('Cokedryll').

The Undercroft, or 'Crypt'

Lying directly below the Chapter House, this was a treasury but is now used as a vestry by the Dean and Chapter. It is not open to the public. The crypt comprises an octagonal chamber with a squat central column and vaulting. It is lit by low windows which can be seen externally at ground level. They were heavily barred to provide high security for the royal treasury in the Middle Ages.

The only other example of an octagonal chapter house standing

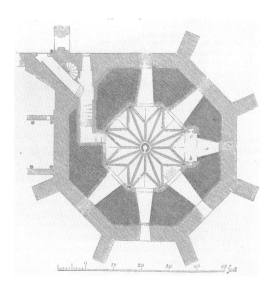

Left: Plan of the undercroft or 'crypt' published in Gleanings from Westminster Abbey *by George Gilbert Scott (1863)*

above a vaulted treasury is at Wells Cathedral, which was copied from Westminster in the 1260s.

THE PYX CHAMBER

The Pyx Chamber, or Chapel of the Pyx, is reached by returning to the cloister and turning left. It is a low, square room with a massive central pillar supporting four bays of vaulting. The chamber was created out of the northern part of the undercroft to the monks' dormitory, built around 1070-80 (the southern part of which is now the Undercroft Museum, run by the Dean and Chapter).

The room takes its unusual name from a ceremony known as the 'Trial of the Pyx'. Pyxes were special boxes in which samples of new coinage were stored while they were waiting to be assayed or tested for purity. The coins were compared with standard specimens called 'Trial Plates' in front of independent witnesses. The trial, which was established in 1281, continued to be held at Westminster Abbey until the nineteenth century, when it was transferred to Goldsmiths' Hall.

The room was separately walled off in the late twelfth century, but it was not until the mid-thirteenth century that it took on the function of a treasury and sacristy, and at this point a stone altar was constructed against the east wall, raised on two steps. Remarkably, that

Engraving of the Pyx chamber from Gleanings from Westminster Abbey

Right: Medieval cope chest, used for storing vestments

The double door at the entrance to the Pyx Chamber

The Pyx Chamber as it appears today with the stone altar against the east wall

altar and the pillar-piscina (basin) alongside it were not destroyed at the Reformation. There are many medieval graffiti on the walls, including masons' marks and several crosses, the latter possibly connected with the consecration of the chapel.

In the early fourteenth century the original access from the vestibule was sealed off and a new doorway opened up in the cloister wall, opposite the altar. A high level of security was clearly demanded, because the opening was fitted with two heavy oak doors, one immediately behind the other. Each door was made of vertical planks sandwiched between 'portcullis' framing on both sides, and was hung on three great strap-hinges. With three locks on each door, six keys were required to gain access. This was one of the most secure treasuries in England.

The floor retains a late thirteenth-century tile pavement, probably laid in 1291. A rectangular outline in the tiling in front of the altar indicates the presence of a single medieval grave. The wooden shelf under the arch to the right of the altar is ancient and of uncertain purpose, but it may have been intended as a place to hold precious caskets. When used as a treasury, the Pyx Chamber would have contained many receptacles, and three massive oak chests of medieval date are still there. The large curved one is a cope chest, which was used for storing vestments laid flat. The others held important treaties and documents of foreign policy, the names of the countries concerned being painted under the lids.